Louisville Scenes

by Caroline Williams

Louisville Scenes

Celestine Vincent

CAROLINE WILLIAMS

DOUBLEDAY & COMPANY, INC.

GARDEN CITY   NEW YORK

1970

*Some of the sketches in this book were
originally published in the Cincinnati* Enquirer

*Library of Congress Catalog Card Number 78-113985
Copyright © 1970 by Caroline Williams
All Rights Reserved
Printed in the United States of America*

FIRST EDITION

Preface

This is a time of sweeping change. Louisville, the city as we have known it for years, seems to be slipping silently away as a new city, more compatible to the times, emerges. All over America urban centers are taking on a new look and Louisville is no exception with plans for redevelopment of mammoth proportions.

This book is a selection of sketches made in and around Louisville and Kentucky at this turning point—not a survey study, not a complete picture in any sense—but a few of the pleasing and meaningful aspects of the city at the start of the Seventies, a time when some of the area is marked for destruction, some already leveled and waiting for giant glass and steel structures to rise in the vacant spaces.

Louisville has always had a flavor all her own, known across the country as a place of charm, with time for hospitality and graciousness; a city on the Ohio River and on the borderline of the North and South, displaying characteristics of both. Soon she will be two hundred years old—a community that has grown slowly but steadily through the years, always leaving a bit of her past as she built for the future. Now when everything moves so fast, it is a sobering thought that what is built today may be around for a long time; that which is demolished can never return again. In the frenetic rush toward a new city, when time-pressured decisions are made in haste, it might be good to look around and hopefully keep some bits and pieces of the past to break the monotony of the modern patterned streets and to remind a new generation of the efforts of those who have gone before and create a happy mixture of the best examples each era has contributed to her growth.

Caroline Williams

Contents

[7]

Foreword

Iɴ ᴛʜᴇ ʏᴇᴀʀ of our next eclipse of the sun, 2024, people in the Louisville area and environs will undoubtedly be searching for an old copy of *Louisville Scenes* by Caroline Williams. With the continued inflation of the American dollar, a first edition of this book, if it can be found then, could easily bring as much as a thousand dollars. Although, sold in limited numbers, perhaps, this book will be around to stay for the centuries. And there is good reason for all of this. Caroline Williams has that one undivided streak of genius. From the time she was a little girl she knew what she wanted to do and she has continued from that time to the present doing it.

Why did her conception of creativity stick to one particular thing? Why did she choose to put old and unique buildings down on her sketch pad? So many years ago, when as a teenage girl she was doing this, she was perhaps smiled on by people who had other, divided dreams, and who tried to cover all, but today they and their creativities are gone and forgotten. Caroline knew what she wanted to do, and she wanted to do it well.

I first became acquainted with Caroline Williams when Annette Patton Cornell was editor of the old and much respected *Talaria Poetry Magazine* and Caroline, then a much younger woman, was doing the illustrations for this magazine. I was one of the contributors when I was a very young man. I knew very little about art, only that which communicated to me. If a poet had a poem in *Talaria* which mentioned a house, there would be an excellent illustration by Caroline Williams, one that would catch the eye, even if the poem fell far below in merit and didn't deserve such illustration. And Caroline Williams did the covers for *Talaria*.

Caroline Williams has today become recognized not only in Louisville and Cincinnati, but nationally and internationally. The Cincinnati and Louisville areas, with small old towns near these major cities, are the background for her art. Her subjects were already here. All she had to do was to use her own artistry in putting them in sketches to last for centuries.

Caroline Williams has a passion for the old architecture from the early beginnings of Louisville and Cincinnati. She weeps when an old building goes. But she has, by premonition, put that old building down onto the artistic page as only Caroline Williams can do, before that building goes. Caroline Williams is the preserver of this rich heritage! And this is where her genius began and this is what has made her an important artist.

Today in Louisville and in Cincinnati, and in other large cities of America, old buildings are coming down. There is such a thing as Urban Renewal, where the old must disappear and the new replace it, where our Federal government assists financially in all this so-called progress. Whole blocks in the hearts of our large cities have come down. Right at the time this book will be published, check your city of Louisville and see how many buildings are coming down! The whole heart of Cincinnati that Caroline Williams has preserved is no more. The old buildings in cities like New York, Washington D.C., Atlanta, New Orleans, and Chicago, just to mention a few, have changed since I was a young man. From the first time I visited these cities until this present time has been approximately thirty-five years. The faces of these and other cities all over America have changed. And who are they who say they have been made more beautiful? Caroline Williams will tell you they haven't! You have an artist in Caroline Williams who would like to clutch the beauty of the past, which has gone and is going with the progress of tomorrow, and hold it to her bosom and never let it die. Since she cannot do this, she has put the beauty of Louisville's past and what is still beautiful into her *Louisville Scenes*.

Here is a book I hope the Louisvillians will buy. It is my belief that this book will be a treasure to have and to hold. It is nice to have today. It will be a collector's item tomorrow.

Knowing what Caroline Williams has done for her part of America, I know generations to be born in the future can learn something of their classic architectural past, something lost from these areas but not forever, by going to their own libraries and getting books by Caroline Williams. In Louisville, they can look up *Louisville Scenes*. And if they are unfortunate enough not to have the book they can go to the Louisville Public Library, one of the finest public libraries in America, where they will find her book.

This remarkable artist has created lovely drawings of homes, stores, public and commercial buildings, churches, schools and bridges in two outstanding and fastest growing cities in the nation. She has caught in her artistic creations the striving for beauty and perfection of the early American architects. She has preserved the best from the early American

[10]

forested land—that which our ancestors met and conquered and on which they did their best to build a world of beauty and greatness. And Americans for the rest of this century and centuries to come will be turning to what she has created. Much of what was once Louisville and some that is still Louisville, that which Caroline Williams has carefully chosen for her art, will not be lost. It is with us and she is one artist whose art will outlive her. It is skillfully made of the edifices, the best created by many men. Caroline Williams is a name that will endure.

Jesse Stuart

Jefferson County Courthouse

L OUISVILLE'S MOST VENERABLE, most impressive building is the Jefferson County courthouse. It is a building a city can take pride in, a representation of its civic past and a nucleus for all future expansion.

The courthouse was built in 1835, and its size tells of the hopes of the small town on the riverbank—the certainty felt for its future growth. The best architect in the state was chosen to create the building—Gideon Shryock, who had designed the capitol in Frankfort five years earlier. It is said that the massive size, much too large for the simple needs of the times, and the dignity of design, were inspired by the burning desire of the City Fathers to have the state seat of government moved here. Beset by money problems, the building was not really completed for twenty four years but it was finished just in time for the one occasion when it did function as the Capitol.

That was in 1862, when General Kirby Smith's Confederate forces were moving from Lexington toward an unprepared Frankfort and the legislature fled to Louisville and its strongly fortified position to convene in the bright new courthouse.

A large bronze statue of Thomas Jefferson stands at the entrance, the patina of age covering the youthful figure on the high pedestal.

Carolin Williams

The Sherman Minton Bridge

When the Sherman Minton Bridge opened in 1962 it was designated the most beautiful long-span bridge of the year by the American Institute of Steel Construction. It is certainly an impressive sight, from the river and from the land, with its great steel arches stretching across the water.

Named for Sherman Minton, Supreme Court Justice from Floyd County, it has added another link to the close tie that has always existed between Kentucky and Indiana. Traffic over the bridge is quite a contrast to the slow travel experienced when people were dependent on little ferry boats to carry them back and forth across the river. No one living today can remember when there were no bridges at all in this area and the difficulties that had to be overcome but, back in the days of the Civil War, boats were lashed together to form a pontoon bridge from Portland to New Albany not only to facilitate moving army supplies but as a speedy means of escape for the citizens if the town was attacked. Now an interstate highway speeds the traffic across the bridge as though no dividing line exists between the cities.

A Covered Bridge

THE LATEST COUNT shows only eighteen covered bridges left in Kentucky. Of these the one at Switzer, in Franklin County, is one of the prettiest. Built in the mid 1800s, the sixty-two foot span, now closed to traffic, crosses the North Fork of Elkhorn Creek.

More nostalgia seems to be aroused by the sight of an old covered bridge than by any other relic of the early days. They are surrounded by a sentimental feeling about the quiet days when there was some leisure, a slower pace and the horse was king of the road. But the old timbered spans are disappearing in spite of great efforts to preserve the last ones left on the little country roads.

And now the old iron spans, one lane, with timbered floors that clatter and vibrate under traffic, are also going fast. The bridges, built in profusion around the turn of the century, proudly bearing name plates of the builders, were found on little roads all over the state not very long ago. Now it is all unadorned concrete, used in more efficient, less picturesque fashion, that crosses the creek beds.

[16]

Walnut Street Baptist Church

From SECOND STREET around Oak, the tall towers of the Walnut Street Baptist Church are seen above the rooftops of the neighborhood which, with the steady march from downtown to the outlying suburbs, has been changing in the last few years.

When the church moved to Third and St. Catherine in 1901, this was not part of downtown Louisville as it is today but a growing suburban area. This was the most fashionable place to live, characterized by large homes, green grass, private schools and clubs, and a concentration of churches—a display of wealth and prosperity which had started in the 1870's.

The church flourishes today in its changing surroundings as it did yesterday in a more quiet atmosphere. The massive, ornate stone building is the largest Baptist Church in the state of Kentucky.

Caroline Williams

Lincoln's Statue

THE LINCOLN STATUE on Fourth Street, by the side of the Public Library, surrounded by trees, is such a familiar memorial that it is seldom noticed by those who pass by.

Memories of Kentucky-born Lincoln are very much a part of Louisville's past. Mementos of his birth and life and family abound. As President during the Civil War when the state of Kentucky was torn apart emotionally, his influence over the citizenry was incalculable.

The admirable statue has often been criticized for the sadness of the facial expression, the gauntness of the figure with rumpled suit and large feet, but it is generally considered a remarkably good interpretation of the man. The original was created by George Grey Barnard in 1917 and stands in Lytle Park in Cincinnati. Two replicas were made; one is in Manchester, England, this one was given to Louisville by Mr. and Mrs. I. W. Bernheim.

Churchill Downs

Louisville, the Kentucky Derby, and Churchill Downs—for some people the three names run together, fused into one inseparable word.

Every year since 1875 when ten thousand people watched Aristides win the first Derby, the city has burst at the seams early in May when horse-lovers, celebrities and thousands of gay spectators come from coast to coast, to see or be seen, to lay down a wager on a favorite or simply to join all the attendant gala festivities.

There has always been horse racing in Louisville. The history books mention it as far back as 1783 when horses were tested for speed on the unpaved dirt streets down by the river. In 1830, Oakland, a real track, was laid out. In the '60s a track and fairgrounds named Woodlawn flourished east of the city.

Then, Churchill Downs opened in 1875, instigated by Colonel M. Lewis who was inspired by the race tracks in England. With interested friends he formed the Kentucky Jockey Club and built the now world-famous course.

Twenty years later a new grandstand was built with the twin towers that have been incorporated into all the more recent enlargements and have become an identifying feature of Churchill Downs.

The University of Louisville

THE UNIVERSITY OF LOUISVILLE is known as the oldest municipal university in the country. It dates back to 1837 when a Medical Institute was established with about eighty students enrolled. This school merged with the Louisville College nine years later and became the University of Louisville, chartered by the general assembly of Kentucky.

In 1924 it moved to the sprawling campus at Third and Shipp Streets and started the steady growth that has made it one of the important educational institutions in the country.

The Administration Building is the nucleus and the most impressive building on the place. At the front steps stands a statue of *The Thinker*, an appropriate symbol for a school. It is not only one of the best-known statues in the world but this particular bronze is of especial value. The Louisville copy is a replica made directly from the original which has stood before the Pantheon in Paris since 1900. It was made in one piece under the direction of the sculptor, Auguste Rodin, himself and sent to the United States by the French Government for its exhibit at the World's Fair in St. Louis. There it was purchased and presented to Louisville by the Hillman-Hopkins family, residents of the city.

The Law School

THE SCHOOL OF LAW at the university, with its impressive list of noted graduates, is outstanding all over the nation. It was established in 1846, the year the university was incorporated, and has grown steadily ever since. For half a century Law and Medicine were the only courses offered by the university which is now made up of many colleges.

The Law School is now housed in one of the first fine buildings erected on Belknap Campus, which is part of the tract of land set apart by the City Council in 1860 for a House of Refuge and a public park. This area was outside the city limits in those days but the corporation line was extended to include the grounds after the Refuge buildings were completed.

When the university took over, several of the old buildings were used until more modern halls could be built. Now the last reminder of the House of Refuge is a small chapel which was converted into a theatre for the dramatic club. It is known simply as the Playhouse.

Caroline Williams

York Street

THERE IS A NEW LOOK around York Street these days where the Eight Hundred Apartments high-rise dwarfs the tower of the old Unitarian Church. For many years the church steeple rose alone against the sky, higher than all the surrounding buildings.

Together, the new glass and steel building and the century-old church compliment each other — forming a pleasing pattern of old and new.

The churches in this edge of downtown Louisville are old. The city grew around them. It was always a quiet section of sedate but lavish residential homes with tree-shaded lawns. Now it is all changing rapidly as business moves in. The houses are being broken up into apartments, parking lots and swank motels are springing up, taking over whole blocks, and the majestic churches are being hemmed in by modern construction.

Caroline Williams

Locust Grove

Locust grove on Blankenbaker Lane is of special interest to visitors in the area not only because of its association with General George Rogers Clark but as an outstanding example of a farm home built as early as 1790.

The house has been restored as nearly as possible to its original state and is furnished in authentic examples of its period, all before 1822. It was built by Major William Croghan and his wife Lucy, General Clark's sister.

It was here that Clark spent the last nine years of his life, dying in 1818 at the age of sixty-six. His later years had been rather tragic. After all his renown as the founder of Louisville, as a general in the Revolution and the man who won the whole Northwest Territory for the nation, his exploits were suddenly over, the war won, the frontier subdued. He lived first in Louisville, then built a home across the river in what is now Clarksville. He was neglected by the government, intemperate, ill, and his leg was finally amputated after an accident. It was then that his sister took him to the pleasant farm house for his last, more peaceful days. This is the only house still standing in which Clark lived.

Cathedral of the Assumption

MODERN BUILDINGS may close in from all sides but the Cathedral of the Assumption will still dominate its area of Fifth Street. The tall spire, rising almost three hundred feet above the sidewalk, is an always familiar feature of the skyline of the city.

The first Catholic church in Louisville was Saint Louis on Main Street, built in 1811. Later a larger building was erected on the present Fifth Street site. When the Roman Catholic see was moved from Bardstown and Louisville became the seat of the Archdiocese embracing Kentucky and Tennessee, Saint Louis was replaced by today's massive Cathedral.

The building was completed in 1852 with the tall spire and the well-known clock which was made in Paris. The enormous bell was presented to the church by Archbishop Bastida of Mexico. Among the treasures inside is a painting of Saint Bernard with the Sacred Host, by an unidentified artist.

Saint Joseph's Proto-Cathedral

When the seat of the Roman Catholic see was moved to Louisville the Cathedral in Bardstown became Saint Joseph's Proto-Cathedral.

From 1808 until that time Bardstown had been the center for the church with the famous Bishop Flaget at the head. The diocese had covered Kentucky and Tennessee, with jurisdiction over the whole Northwest Territory.

The beautiful building was dedicated in 1819 and is the oldest Cathedral west of the Alleghenies. It must have been a magnificent achievement for the tiny pioneer community. Three years of work had gone into its construction. The timbers and woodwork, as well as the poplar columns in the front, were cut from the trees in the surrounding forests, the bricks burned on the place, the limestone quarried nearby.

The building is famous for its valuable paintings and lavish furnishings. It is said that some of the treasures were gifts from Louis Philippe, Duke of Orléans and later King of France, sent to the church thirty years after he had stopped over in Bardstown and was befriended by the church people.

Bridges from Jeffersonville

IT WAS AN EPOCHAL EVENT when Kentucky and Indiana were joined by the first bridge over the Ohio River in 1870. That was the Fourteenth Street Railway Bridge, and it created the first direct commercial link between the North and South, an inestimable boon to transportation.

Now, the many bridges in the area furnish speedy intercourse, the two interstate highway spans speeding the through traffic on across the country.

From Jeffersonville, the newest of the bridges, the John Fitzgerald Kennedy Memorial Bridge, looms high. Finished in 1964, it stands close by the older George Rogers Clark Bridge which carries its share of traffic across the water that divides the two states.

Caroline Williams

The City Hall and Court House

I T COMES AS SOMETHING of a shock to realize that the City Hall has reached its century mark. For so many years the contrast has been drawn between the ornate building and the simple lines of the Court House, always mentioned as representative of the very old and the newer of the civic buildings. The difference in age is still there — 1870 for the new; the old started in 1835 — but now they are both venerable old-timers waiting to enhance all the modern structures put up nearby.

The two buildings have always complimented each other by their differences in architectural décor and serve as interesting examples of the continuity of history and the growth of the city.

Caroline Williams

The Old Capitol – Frankfort

THE FINE OLD state house in Frankfort was built in 1830, designed by Gideon Shryock, a young man of twenty-five who immediately became the most renowned architect in Kentucky. The building is of marble, hand-quarried from the bluffs of the Kentucky River. Its pure copper dome and massive columns, its sedate and simple dignity, make it one of the most admired buildings in the State.

Frankfort was the first state capital created west of the Alleghenies. The small town was given this honor in 1792 in spite of Lexington and Louisville, larger communities which bid determinedly for the title and continued to work to have it moved until 1892 when the constitution made Frankfort officially and permanently the capital.

Frankfort was also the only capital loyal to the Union captured by the Confederates during the Civil War. It was seized by Kirby Smith in September of 1862 but retaken by the Union forces one month later, just as the rebel government was installing Richard Hawes as governor.

The building served until 1910 when the new state house was built. Now it is the headquarters and museum of the Kentucky Historical Society. Apart from the many displays, the building itself stands as a valuable historic relic inside and out. One of the attractions is the double marble stairway that circles upward from the center hall with no obvious means of support. It is unique in all the world.

Caroline Williams

Perryville

Louisville, a border city with deep ties to both the North and the South, was deeply affected by the Civil War but it was never attacked and did not suffer as seriously as many places nearby.

On the Mackville Pike a few miles out of Perryville, there is a small park which marks the spot where the biggest and bloodiest battle in Kentucky was fought. There is a monument to the Union dead but the Confederate memorial, erected in 1902, is more conspicuous. As one looks up, he sees the foreshortened soldier atop the tall shaft, seeming too small, his gun a toy, his hat too big. The statue might be called quaintly amusing. The battle it commemorates was not. Words cannot describe the horror of the action on that autumn day in 1862. All the casualty figures of the Civil War seem almost unbelievable today, those of the battle of Perryville, so close to home, in such a quiet spot, seem impossible.

The two armies, under General Braxton Bragg and General Don Carlos Buell, met almost by accident and in one afternoon, on this small tract of peaceful farm land, there were almost eight thousand casualties with one thousand three hundred and fifty-five soldiers killed before the night fell. And neither side could claim a victory. The Confederates counted the fewer losses but retreated during the night, leaving the field to the Union army. This ended the Southern campaign to gain possession of Kentucky.

Caroline Williams

First Christian Church

THE FIRST CHRISTIAN CHURCH extends around the corner of Fourth and Breckinridge, an imposing, massive structure that adds greatly to the beauty of the neighborhood.

The Christian Church has a long history in the annals of the city for it was around 1835 that a new religious body, the Disciples of Christ, was formed in Louisville. It was created from the membership of the Reformed Baptist Church which, in turn, had separated from the First Baptist.

The new congregation built its first church building on Second Street between Market and Jefferson, later moving to Fourth and Walnut. With this move the name was changed to the Walnut Street Christian Church, a name retained until 1870 when it became officially the First Christian Church.

The present fine building was dedicated in 1911. Now, as a downtown church, along with the other nearby churches, it is deeply involved in neighborhood projects and social programs.

Caroline Williams

The Fort Nelson Building

I<small>F ANYONE</small> has the time to look up—or dares take his eyes off the traffic that roars by on Main Street—he will find that the top of the Fort Nelson Building adds an interesting touch to the skyline.

The building, west of the Monument to Fort Nelson, is not in itself of especial historic or architectural value. It is simply that in this day of glass and steel construction, unbroken surfaces and the monotonous sameness of façades, it is a pleasure sometimes to look up at a fanciful bit of decoration from an earlier era and see how some individualistic builder wanted the top of his creation to look.

An Old House
on Lampton Street

Ghosts of lost grandeur must haunt this old house on Lampton Street. It stands forlorn and neglected but still showing signs of its more prosperous early days. Well built, simple in design, it is typical of its period of the 1840s. There are few examples of that time left downtown, now that the Benjamin Smith house, and the famous Grayson home are gone, as well as the later Ford Mansion, used as the YWCA for years, and the old Newcomb place.

In 1840 the town had a population of around thirty thousand, concentrated along the river and expanding slowly. Lampton Street was in a section that was practically in the country, with widely scattered houses on large acreage, built by people of wealth who wanted homes indicative of their opulence. Now this house stands in a crowded neighborhood, closed in by smaller, newer homes. Years ago it lost its status as a private residence and became a Masonic Hall. It seems to be a house with a bleak future and only a memory of a past.

Caroline Williams

The City Hall Annex

O<small>N JEFFERSON STREET</small>, the City Hall Annex contributes to the variety and continuity of the architectural styles represented by the public buildings. It has almost too much of a lavish massiveness; the ornate columns are rather overwhelming. With the other buildings it helps make a display of the taste and styles of the various years represented—the Annex of 1910 with its opulence; next door the City Hall's postbellum intricacies of 1870; and both overshadowed by the restrained dignity of the old Court House designed in 1838.

When the Annex was new its most important offices were occupied by the Sinking Fund Commission and for some years the place was known simply as the Sinking Fund Building.

McAlpine Locks and Dam

THE GIANT, modern McAlpine Locks and Dam are the result of a continuity of effort that goes back to the very birth of the town.

This is the final solution to the problem created by the swift rapids in the river which are always referred to as the "Falls of the Ohio." They were the only falls in the entire length of the Ohio; the present facilities, which left only a fossil bed to mark their existence, is the biggest dam and lock complex in the nine hundred and eighty-one miles of river.

From the time the first settlers landed at Corn Island, then moved to the shore to start a permanent settlement, the falls were the major obstacle for navigation. Through those first struggling years the cargoes on the river boats were unloaded, carried across land, then reloaded, above or below the falls. Then, in 1830, the Portland Canal, after years of work, was finished and the problem eased.

The system has been under constant improvement and enlargement ever since. In 1930, just a century after the canal was opened, today's basic dam and hydroelectric plant were completed. The complex was known as Lock and Dam 41 for thirty years. Then the name was changed to honor W. H. McAlpine, the only civilian to hold the title of district engineer in the Corps' Louisville District.

In 1964, after further massive improvements, the present giant complex opened a new era in navigation. Three locks of various size easily handle boats of all description from the smallest to the largest. People say it handles more annual traffic than the Gatun Lock for the Panama Canal. It is all rather mysteriously fascinating.

Caroline Williams

Temple Adath Israel

TEMPLE ADATH ISRAEL, with its adjoining educational building, extends along the block between York and Breckinridge on Third Street —a stately symbol of religious dignity.

The Jewish community of Louisville has played an important role in all aspects of the cultural progress of the city since the first congregation was formed in 1842. There are now five congregations but Adath Israel is the only one still located in the downtown section.

Jeffersonville

JEFFERSONVILLE has a wonderfully scenic river front. The unobstructed view of the water extends for several miles, and Riverside Drive, with boat docks and fishermen, is about as peaceful and pleasant as any spot could be.

Jeffersonville is an old town. It was laid out and named in 1802 by William Henry Harrison but it goes back even farther—to Fort Steuben and the settlement made here in 1786, opposite the equally tiny settlement of Louisville just across the way. Today it is an independent, thriving city closely allied with the metropolitan area that spreads across the river and includes both Indiana and Kentucky.

Among the historic buildings of the city is its oldest house at Market and Pearl. This was built in 1815 and owned by John Zulauf, president of an early railroad.

C. Williams

Caroline Williams

Farmington

THE BEAUTIFUL Jeffersonian house on Bardstown Road, known as Farmington, dates back to 1810. It was built by John and Lucy Fry Speed on a fifteen hundred acre land grant signed by Patrick Henry. All this was a wilderness then. Louisville itself wasn't very large—as one visitor, an Englishman named Cuming, wrote in 1808: "Louisville consists of one principal and very handsome street, about a mile long, tolerably compactly built . . ."

The local builder of the place followed plans drawn by Thomas Jefferson in designing the fourteen room house and today it stands as a representative example of the best of its period, from its octagonal rooms and fanlighted doorways to its hidden stairway. The furnishings are antiques all made prior to 1820.

In a time of gracious living, the fine old home housed an interesting family. Judge Speed and his wife had ten children, among them Joshua, who was one of Abraham Lincoln's closest friends, and James who served as Attorney General during Lincoln's second administration. The President was but one of the famous guests known to have visited the Louisville estate.

It is now owned and has been restored by Historic Homes Foundation.

An Old Mill

ONCE, a mill was just a place of business, necessary but not unusual. The water wheel was part of the mechanism. Mills were found in every hamlet scattered through the countryside, wherever the water was available and farmers had grain to grind into meal.

Now they are so scarce, so hard to find, that reproductions are put up to show a new generation one aspect of an earlier life.

One of the most picturesque mills still standing in Kentucky, and one of the oldest, is the Wolf Pen Mill near Harrods Creek. The stone building and overshot wheel date back a hundred and thirty years or more.

Caroline Williams

Catherine Spalding College

CATHERINE SPALDING COLLEGE, which was created in 1920 with an enrollment of forty girls, is now a co-educational school of more than fifteen hundred students with seven modern buildings to serve their needs.

The popular school was established as Nazareth College by the Sisters of Charity of Nazareth, Kentucky. For their home they bought the mansion built by Joseph T. Thompkins on Fourth Street, a beautiful place with elaborate carvings, paneling and furnishings, designed after the Civil War by the famous local architect, Henry Whitestone and built in this fashionable neighborhood noted for its extravagant homes.

The house is still the core of the Administration Building although its exterior has disappeared as more and more additions and enlargements have been made. Inside it remains the heart of the place, with the old drawing room, dining room and stairway still in use.

Caroline Williams

Saint Anthony Church

THE LACY, slender spire of Saint Anthony Church rises high above the roof tops in the old West End. The venerable church, on Market and Twenty-third Streets is truly a landmark, visible from many miles around.

The congregation held its centennial in 1967, celebrating the opening of its first church. The present fine building replaced the smaller stone edifice twenty years later. The tall spire was added in 1904.

The parish, established to serve the many German families that lived in the West End, has had many troublesome times. Their church and their homes were damaged by the great flood of 1937. Things had just returned to normal when a disastrous fire of unknown origin swept through the buildings, completely destroying the interior but leaving the sturdy walls and spire standing. It seems, however, that members of the parish did not lose their sense of humor. In the records are a few lines written at the time by a parishioner titled, "Hell and High Water":

> *"High water first and then our hell*
> *Our church in ruins quickly fell*
> *We thought high water such a curse*
> *But decided fire could be much worse."*

Two years later the church, rebuilt, opened again, more beautiful than ever although the marble which now graces the sanctuary and which had been ordered sometime before was delayed by World War II. The marble lay hidden in a field in Italy all through the conflict and was not delivered until 1946.

Federal Hill – Bardstown

P<small>ROBABLY</small> the best known house in Kentucky, and the one with the widest appeal outside the state, is Federal Hill. The brick mansion, built by John Rowan on a great plantation near Bardstown, was completed in 1818 but what is now the rear wing is the original house on the place and was built twenty-three years earlier.

The Rowens were interesting people. John Rowen, who started the estate, was a Secretary of State, Congressman, judge of the Court of Appeals, and finally a United States Senator. His son was United States Minister to Naples. However it is not their importance, the charm or the age of the building, that has made the house so popular. It is famous and is indelibly identified with the Rowens' cousin, Stephen Collins Foster and "My Old Kentucky Home." It is believed that this old place, which he visited, was the inspiration for that enduringly popular song.

Nearby stands a small log room, built over a stone spring house, which was used as Rowen's law office. Here he trained young lawyers as well as welcoming established and celebrated members of the bar.

Union Station

THERE IS A DEFINITE FEELING of nostalgia, a sentimental aura, around a railroad station for anyone old enough to remember when a train was the monarch of travel. Today, planes, buses, and, most of all individual cars, have replaced passenger trains, and a railroad station, once a hub of activity twenty-four hours of the day, is a lonesome ghost of its past.

The Union Station down on Broadway is typical, lavishly built in the 1880s when trains were at the height of their days of glory. It was one of the busiest places in town.

Louisville had one of the first railroads in the United States—a little train that ran between this city and Lexington in the early 1830s. By the 1860s the railroads were becoming commercially competitive, taking the freight hauling business as well as the passengers away from the steamboats. Before long eight lines were coming into the city with industrial plants building close by the tracks.

Now, with passenger service at a low ebb and stations sparsely frequented, the future of these large, elaborate buildings in the midst of modern cities is in doubt.

Christ Church Cathedral

T HE OLDEST CHURCH in Louisville is Christ Church Cathedral, built in 1822. It was consecrated as the Cathedral in 1894.

Louisville was just a small town, with plenty of space and no tall buildings, when the church was built on Second Street. Now the city has grown up around it. It is closed in by business houses, motels, service stations and parking lots. Its former congregation has moved farther out to the suburbs and many problems arise from the changing surroundings.

Originally the church was just a one-story building, almost square. In 1872 the front wall was removed and the building extended forward, the two towers added. That is the way it has remained, an interesting downtown landmark all tied in with the city's history, and Cathedral for the Episcopal Diocese of Kentucky.

Carolina Williams

The Haymarket

An OUTDOOR MARKET, where farmers sell their products to the space-cramped city dwellers, is about the earliest form of retail, cash and carry trading that there is. As soon as Louisville became a crowded little town, with limited garden space, it had a market. It is known that as early as 1804 a block long open market flourished between Fourth and Fifth Streets on the thoroughfare which later became known as Market Street. One must assume that is how the street received its name.

Today, the Haymarket on West Jefferson Street is a popular and well-patronized institution. It was started about ninety years ago when farmers, coming to town with their fresh produce to sell—including hay—gathered together in an abandoned railroad yard to spread out their offerings. When the expanding city began taking over the area for new buildings some of the farmers formed a stock company which purchased its own space for a permanent market. Here stalls are rented and the fresh fruit and vegetables from far and near are displayed under an extensive roof. In the very early morning, wholesalers swarm over the place. Later in the day the householders from all around the city come to pick and choose and buy in smaller quantities from the colorful, enticing miscellany.

Scribner House, New Albany

New ALBANY, seat of Floyd County, Indiana, and right across the river from Louisville, takes great pride in its combination of old and new; in restoring its historic structures while developing new enterprises in sparkling modern buildings.

New Albany's early history is linked with the Ohio River. For many years almost all of its industry was dependent on the boats that had made this a key riverport as they traveled up and down between Pittsburgh and New Orleans. It became a thriving ship building center and was the largest town in Indiana through this period.

Like Louisville, the site for the city was chosen by the first settlers because of the falls in the Ohio. It was in 1813 that three enterprising brothers from the east saw the possibilities of the location, bought eighty-six and a half acres and platted a town. They named it for Albany, New York. They were Joel, Nathaniel and Abner Scribner, and two years later Joel built himself a home on Main Street. This, well preserved, is now the oldest house in town. For contrast, from the side, the graceful arch of the modern Sherman Minton Bridge can be seen spanning the broad river. The place is now headquarters for the Piankeshaw Chapter of the Daughters of the American Revolution.

The Old Clock Tower
—New Albany

For some time New Albany has been involved in a campaign to restore its historic buildings and retain the pleasing flavor of the old river town that she has always been. In this effort, the mellowed bricks of the old town church have been renovated and the trim painted a gleaming white.

Everyone knows the old church on Main Street. The steeple rises high above the buildings in the lower part of town, the four clock faces on its sides have been telling passers by the time for over a century.

Some of the mansions of the mid 1800s have been restored and filled with authentic furnishings of the period, others renovated. Through the streets roams a replica of a steamboat—built on the chassis of a bus. It is the *Robert E. Lee* bus, named for the city's most famous boat, a magnificent floating palace which won the historic race against the *Natchez* in the golden days of river traffic.

Along Main Street, flaming copper gas lights line the center of the downtown plaza.

Fort Knox

AT FORT KNOX, the United States Government doesn't let anyone see that gold that everyone knows is there. In fact, the guards won't even let you get close to the building erected in 1936 to house the gleaming mint bars. A fence—and it's live—surrounds the granite, concrete and steel fortress, but a firm voice over a loudspeaker stops the tourist at the entrance which is about a block away on Bullion Boulevard.

They say about a quarter of a million tourists enter the grounds each year and that the biggest attraction on the post is the gold depository, but guarding the money is not the main function of this base. Located about thirty miles south of Louisville, it is one of the largest military installations in the nation. It has been growing since 1903 when part of the area was used for the first time for Army maneuvers. Fifteen years later forty thousand acres were purchased and a permanent base established. It was named for Major General Henry Knox of Revolutionary War fame. Now around sixty thousand military and civilian personnel are garrisoned on an area covering some hundred and ten thousand acres.

Caroline Williams

Guthrie Street

GUTHRIE IS A NAME that recurs again and again in the early annals, for James Guthrie was the leading figure in Democratic politics in his time, an influential man.

In today's city, the name is remembered by one short street, just two blocks long, that runs from Second to Fourth between Walnut and Chestnut.

Guthrie owned property around here; his home was at the corner of Second and Walnut. That was when he was leading the campaign to make Louisville the state capitol; the time the courthouse was being built —"Guthrie's folly" as it was called, because his faith in making it the state house was instrumental in planning a building out of proportion to the size of the small city. Later he was Secretary of the Treasury under President Pierce and president of the L.&N. railroad.

Caroline Williams

Calvary Episcopal Church

IN THE RECORDS of Calvary Episcopal Church it is stated that "nothing was spared to build a church unsurpassed in elegance and beauty." The remark was written a century ago when the large stone building on Fourth Street was new. The small congregation had almost over-reached its ability to pay for such a lavish structure and it was several years before the beautiful church it had planned was really completed.

Calvary was established in 1860 and struggled through the turbulent days of the Civil War. After peace was assured the Fourth Street site was purchased and the cornerstone laid in 1872. At the time this was becoming the most fashionable neighborhood in town as the city was pushing its residential section southward. Calvary, along with the First Unitarian on the corner of York, were the first of the many churches built among the new homes.

St. James Court

A REMNANT OF THE GAS LIGHT ERA, a delightful oasis in the city, St. James Court, refurbished and serene, offers a glimpse into the opulent period of Louisville's early 1900s.

In 1883 this was the site of the fabulous Southern Exposition, when about forty acres of land just south of and including Central Park were taken over for the magnificent fair, remembered as one of the city's most enterprising endeavors. The Exposition, opened by President Chester A. Arthur and visited by thousands, opened each summer for five years, then the land was put up for sale. The Victoria Land Company purchased this tract and under the direction of W. H. Slaughter designed the Court. Modeled after the residential parks of London and lined with linden and horse chestnut trees, it was secluded, quiet, and fashionable.

Slaughter imported the delicate fountain, with its graceful nymph, water sprites and swans, which continues to dominate the center of the pleasant neighborhood.

Many of the homes are now apartments and clubhouses but restored and carefully maintained, this gas lit area offers a step into the past in the midst of a hurrying city.

Caroline Williams

A House on
St. James Court

ONE OF THE interesting houses on St. James Court was once the home of Owen Tyler who wase Chairman of the Board of Aldermen and served as acting Mayor from 1905 to 1907.

It is typical of the neighborhood only in that it is lavish and individual. Houses are not alike on the Court; each has its own identity. Many are elaborate, and they are all tastefully dignified. They are beautiful places—some of the finest examples of Victorian elegance found anywhere. The lovely trees, green grass and gas lights all add charm to this section.

The Court was a favorite of professional people, artists and writers when it was new. Among the residents were Cale Young Rice and his wife Alice Hegan Rice, the author. Her classic *Mrs. Wiggs of the Cabbage Patch* was inspired by a little community nearby that had developed along the railroad tracks.

When W. H. Slaughter, who built the first house on the street, brought over the fountain that stands in the center of the Court, he also imported four iron lions, placing two at each entrance. Now only two are left—one at each end—serving as benign and sleepy looking guardians.

Church of Our Lady

PORTLAND is now just a part of the western end of the city, just a whisper of its former self when it was a lusty, growing, separate community rivaling Louisville. One town was below the Falls, the other above, and the freight carried by the river boats portaged back and forth between the two.

In 1828, when Louisville was incorporated, Portland refused to be included, keeping its separate identity for nine more years. Finally a road was built between the two, then a little railroad linked them even closer together. When the canal was built, Portland's independence was doomed though it continued to thrive for years as a favorite residential area for the river people, pilots, steamboat captains and shippers.

Our Lady, Notre Dame du Port, Church is one of the few landmarks of those earlier days. It dates back to 1839 when a pastor was sent from Bardstown and the parish was established—a parish embracing all the territory bounded by the present Dixie Highway, the Ohio River and south to West Point, Kentucky. A small building at Rudd Street and Cedar Grove was soon put up, the hundred and fifty thousand bricks needed made from the clay on the lot, all the timbers, flooring, window frames and pews cut from the trees felled on the grounds. The steeple and belfrey were added in 1850. The present building which still has the original steeple and is constructed with the same bricks, was built in 1873.

Caroline Williams

Statue of King Louis XVI

I F A CITY is named for a king, it should certainly have a token reminder of the monarch. Louisville now, after all these years, has one—a thirteen-ton marble statue of King Louis XVI standing on the west lawn of the courthouse.

It was in May of 1780 that the Virginia Legislature divided Kentucky County, created Jefferson County, and "established the town of Louisville." The name was a gesture of gratitude to France, honoring its king for the invaluable aid his country had provided in the Revolution. For some years the settlement was so small that the words, "Falls of the Ohio," were added to further identify the place.

There seem to be no records that the King made any gesture toward his namesake, and the city progressed for years with no great acknowledgment of its pleasure. History has never been overly kind to the Bourbon Monarch, beheaded at the age of thirty-nine, but now with the softening of time, he is just a story-book figure in a far-off age and it is very pleasant indeed to have the statue at long last, a very fitting relic of Louisville's history.

The statue is over a hundred and fifty years old and was in storage for most of that time. It was presented to Louisville by Montpellier, her sister city in France, in 1967, and dedicated with a ceremony attended by the mayor of Montpellier and a delegation from that town as well as the French Ambassador to the United States. In Carrara marble, the rather pudgy figure, with its pedestal, stands in majesty seventeen feet above the ground. No explanation can be found for the child reclining at his feet.

Caroline Williams.

The Fort Nelson Monument

I T IS NOT very beautiful but at least there is a memorial tablet to mark the site of Fort Nelson and the beginning of the city. It was here, at present day Seventh and Main, encompassing about an acre of ground spreading North to the river, that George Rogers Clark, in 1782, built the defensive military base for his little band of soldiers and a place of refuge for the first settlers.

Twenty families had come along with the general and his hundred and fifty men as they journeyed forth to win the Northwest from the British in 1778. Before proceeding onward, he settled the group of civilians above the falls on Corn Island, now covered by water, with instructions to move to the mainland for the winter. By Fall they had built a fort near the foot of what is now Twelfth Street.

After Clark returned from his victorious campaign he built a more permanent, larger fort nearby, naming it for Governor Thomas Nelson of Virginia. It was considered the strongest fortification in the West and offered protection to the rapidly increasing band of pioneers who were gradually spreading out and around its confines and beginning to build a town along the river.

The irregular slab of granite with the bronze tablet was erected by the Colonial Dames of America in 1912.

To Commemorate
The Establishment
of the Town of
Louisville 1780
...

Caroline Williams

Jefferson Community College

Jefferson community college occupies the most attractive group of buildings on Broadway. New buildings are being added, seven modern structures planned for the eight acre campus, but the nucleus of the school is the old Presbyterian Theological Seminary acquired by the city in 1965.

The Seminary, noted for its beauty, consisted of several halls, built of limestone and arranged in an open quadrangle entered through the ornate stone gates on Broadway. The courtyard is surrounded by the battlemented walls of the buildings, pierced with slender gothic windows with delicate traceries. The place was inspired by colleges at Oxford, England.

The Community College is representative of the new era in higher education. A two year program is designed to function as a valued link in the whole chain of learning. It is part of the University of Kentucky tied in with the University of Louisville through a joint executive commission as an advisory group.

Caroline Williams

Heigold House Front

Many cities have preserved old houses for posterity. Louisville has dared to be different—it has preserved the front of a house—and an interesting memento it is. When it was whole it was the Heigold house and stood on Marion Street. It was moved to River Road through the efforts of a few concerned citizens.

The story is that Charles Heigold, an immigrant from Germany, a stonecutter who installed the steps of the courthouse, was building himself a house during the infamous days of the Know-Nothing Party, when "foreigners" were looked upon with suspicion by many. Disturbed by the sentiment around him and filled with patriotism for his new country, he carved his feelings all over the front of his house, around and over the windows and door. He started in 1857 and spent nine years chiseling away at his project.

There is a small bust of Washington, surrounded by a coat of arms. There is a larger bust of President James Buchanan with the words "His virtues and patriotism entitles him to a crown of laurel from the gratitude of his people." There are heroic figures with swords and shields, torches and olive branches, there are wreaths, cannons and stars, garlands and words of wisdom... "Hail to the City of Louisville.... Hail to the Union—Never Dissolve it... Hail to all men of the U. States."

After the house had stood as a curiosity for almost a century, a city land-fill dump project found it in its path. Protesting citizens saved it from total destruction so it sat amidst the rubble for three years, used as an office for the workmen. Vandals and neglect took their toll and in 1953 the city was persuaded to take down the front—in three hundred and fifteen pieces—and erect it again in Thurston Park, where it stands as one of the more pleasant mementos of a bygone day. The man was no renown architect but he worked with zeal and enthusiasm—it is something that brings a smile to a serious world, and a smile with a patriotic stone mason might well be more valuable than cold admiration for an austere work of art.

Caroline Williams

Daniel Boone Statue

THE LEGENDARY STORIES of the exploits of Daniel Boone never portray him as a modest man. Possibly he knew he was destined to become a heroic figure symbolizing the pioneer, his name to be forever synonymous with Kentucky.

There were giants among the pioneers who came into a wilderness and turned it into a state — men like James Harrod, Ben Logan and the fascinating George Rogers Clark. They were rugged builders, tough and determined settlers, but it was the scout, the pathfinder, the backwoods fighter, who has come out of the past as the best known of them all.

So Louisville has his statue — bigger than life — guarding the Eastern Parkway entrance to Cherokee Park. It is a fine statue, free-swinging, designed by the city's own Enid Yandell. A pupil of Rodin in Paris, the gifted sculptor has many representative works in the local area. This one was done originally in plaster of Paris for the Kentucky exhibit at the Chicago World's Fair. Later it was cast in bronze and purchased by C. C. Bickel as a gift to the city in 1906.

Cherokee Park, many acres of rolling hillsides, is one of the oldest parks laid out by Louisville. One of the familiar features is a stone bridge that crosses the Middle Fork of Beargrass Creek as it meanders through the park.

Caroline Williams

The Coast Guard Station

Down at the waterfront — at the end of Third Street — is the only inland Coast Guard Station in the United States. Established in 1881 it holds an impressive record in saving lives from the Ohio River.

The Coast Guard is located at a spot teeming with history. This was the entrance to the City when its life centered around the River. Upstream is Towhead Island, the stopping point for boats that were to be towed around the Falls, their cargoes hauled overland. Downstream is one end of the Louisville and Portland Canal that later made the portage unnecessary. The mouth of Beargrass Creek has been moved a few miles upstream but it originally entered the river around here, between Third and Fourth Streets, forming a natural harbor, one of the best on the river. Here Bullitt camped when he came to Kentucky in 1773, as a Virginia surveyor, and determined this as the likely site for the town later named Louisville.

Carolin Williams

Shelbyville

NEARBY SHELBYVILLE has close ties with Louisville which date back to the infancy of the two settlements. Shelbyville developed from the little fort at Painted Stone built in the wilderness by Squire Boone, brother of Daniel. For a time this little shelter was the only refuge for travelers on the trail between the two stronger forts that had been built at Harrodsburg and Louisville.

Squire Boone was a preacher as well as frontiersman and is said to have delivered the first Baptist sermon given in the settlement by the Falls.

Shelbyville has grown up now. It is a busy, bustling town but it hasn't forgotten its history. There is a modern courthouse, built in 1912, but a replica of a blockhouse stands across the street in a little park. It is not a pioneer fort from Boone's day but represents a rather unique method of combating crime back in 1858. At that time the place was being harassed by gangs of guerrillas who were raiding the town. So, right in the middle of an intersection of Main Street, they put up a blockhouse, pierced with little holes through which to shoot. When the alarm sounded the townsmen rushed in, safe but ready. The refuge was torn down in 1870 when law and order had been restored but several years ago the town erected this rough log replica near its original site.

Third Street From Liberty

As LONG AS anyone can remember, the clock on the Chamber of Commerce Building at the corner of Third and Liberty has extended out over the sidewalk, registering the minutes and hours. The huge time piece dominates the view of Third Street, where old buildings mingle with the new, ranging in age from the modern Methodist Trinity Temple in the distance to the Chamber of Commerce Building itself.

The Chamber occupies the old building that housed the *Courier-Journal* and the Louisville *Times* from 1919 to 1948. The four story limestone building was put up by the United States Government as a Post Office and Federal Building in 1858, when Liberty Street was still known as Green.

Old Bank of Louisville

For many people the Old Bank of Louisville on Main Street is the most pleasing building in town. It looks like a bank and it too was designed by Gideon Shryock who has given us some of the finest buildings in Kentucky, locally the giant Court House and the old college on Chestnut.

Possibly because it is the smallest of his buildings, it is the most impressive, the simple ornamentation on top the most easily appreciated. A gem of a building, erected in 1837, it stands proudly among the taller structures that surround it, nicely preserved by the Credit Men's Association, the present owners.

A House on Brook Street

I<small>T WAS</small> around the middle of the last century that ornamental "iron fronts" for houses were at the height of their popularity. Stairways, balconies, porches and fences enhanced the entrances of many homes, the intricate filigree patterns adding charm to simple brick houses, as well as mansions.

Some of the decorative trimmings were imported, but after ore was found in the Ohio River bluffs, iron works flourished in Kentucky, attracting skilled artisans from Europe who duplicated the foreign designs with great taste. Much of their work was sent to New Orleans.

Reproductions of metal ornamentation are very much in style again today but there are still excellent examples of the original work in Louisville. One is the extensive porch on a fine house on Brook Street that was built in 1858 by John D. Green. At that time it was surrounded by spacious grounds, part of the acreage that had been known as Jacobs' Woods in the old days, a tract of uncultivated land that fronted on Broadway and was owned by John I. Jacobs. Here the early townspeople gathered to celebrate national holidays, like the Fourth of July, with picnics and speeches and fireworks.

Now the lovely house, on a busy city street, serves as headquarters for the Catholic Charities Agency.

Caroline Williams

Fourth Avenue United Methodist Church

THE MASSIVE STONE building of the Fourth Avenue Methodist Church, gracing the corner of Fourth Street and St. Catherine, is a familiar and beloved landmark in the central city area.

The early Methodists of Louisville organized their first congregation in 1806 and purchased a lot on Market Street between Seventh and Eighth for their building. It was the first denominational church in town. As the city grew and the membership increased, newer and larger buildings were erected.

In 1888 part of the congregation of this old church combined with members from the Chestnut Street Church and formed the Fourth Avenue Methodist which erected as their home the present beautiful building.

Grayson House

ONE OF LOUISVILLE's most interesting houses was the Gwathney, or the Grayson, house, as it was usually known. The three-story home on Sixth near Walnut was built by John Gwathney in 1810, or even earlier according to some historians. It passed into the hands of the Frederick Graysons a few years later.

It was sturdily built with detailed care. The bricks were not made on the place, as was the custom in those days, but were laboriously brought down the river on keelboats from the East. On the site of an ancient Indian mound, the house stood slightly elevated, with the servants' quarters occupying the first floor and outside steps leading to the seventeen family rooms above.

In its final days it was just a house on a busy street but originally the surrounding extensive grounds led down to "Grayson's Lake," a fashionable gathering place for parties and picnics in the summer, ice skating in the winter.

Caroline Williams

Harrodsburg

IT WAS AT Fort Harrod that George Rogers Clark planned his march into the old Northwest, an expedition which led to the settlement of Louisville. Harrodsburg was established four year before he brought his little band of pioneers to Corn Island.

It was in 1773 that James Harrod, one of the surveyors looking over the territory for the Governor of Virginia, selected the site for his fort. The next year he returned with thirty one men and the first cabins were built. This was the first permanent settlement in all Kentucky.

Now a reconstruction of the original fort marks the spot. It is a token recognition that here were recorded so many first events in the history of Kentucky—here the first school was held; the first court of justice convened; the first corn raised; the first white child born.

At the entrance to the fort, and within the palisades, is a small brick building known as the Lincoln Marriage Temple. Inside, protected from the weather, is the rough-hewn log cabin in which Nancy Hanks and Thomas Lincoln were married in 1806. The cabin was moved here from the nearby Beech Fork Settlement.

Carolin Williams

The Mud Meeting House

O NE OF THE FEW pioneer churches still standing in Kentucky is the Mud Meeting House in Mercer County. The first Dutch Reformed Church west of the Alleghenies, it dates all the way back to 1800 when a congregation formed four years earlier purchased the land on Dry Branch Pike.

The place is valued not only for its age but as an almost unique example of pioneer construction. The outside is now covered with weatherboard, but the unusual materials and methods of building can be seen from the inside. Upright, squared timbers were attached to heavy log sills, pieces of hand-split hickory were mortised horizontally across the timbers then clay mixed with straw was packed in tight, forming the solid mud walls which gave the church its name.

The original congregation had moved into this sparsely settled wilderness from Pennsylvania and New Jersey. As more pioneers arrived and more churches were built, the congregation was gradually absorbed by the more popular religious organizations. Finally the building was taken over by the Presbyterians who met here for many years.

In 1928 the Dutch Reformed Church of America presented the deed to the old place to the Harrodsburg Historical Society and it has been preserved as one of the interesting relics of the past.

The Old Pumping Station

WHEN TRAVELING along the River Road, one sees a tall white shaft suddenly appear in the distance, a giant monument against the sky. The structure is familiar to the local people, but strangers are surprised to learn that it is the tower of the century-old Pumping Station for the Louisville Water Company.

It is the most elaborate bit of construction anyone could imagine for such a utilitarian purpose. And all this was done when the company had only five hundred and twelve customers.

The place was built, at Zorn Avenue, in pre-Civil War days when the Greek Revival style of architecture was at the height of its popularity. It consists of several buildings, startlingly white, with an effusion of design. It is the tower, however, that is the most interesting. The top is in the form of a giant lantern while the circular base is surrounded by a series of fluted, decorative columns topped by ten statues.

The statues cause the most comment. There are nine classic figures of mythical gods and goddesses—Neptune, of course, Mercury, Vesta, and others, and then the tenth is one lone Indian—with a dog. That Indian has been a cause of much puzzlement and speculation through the years. It is now decided that, when several of the figures were blown from their heights in a cyclone in 1890, one was beyond repair and was replaced with our Indian. Where he came from, no one knows, since a local monument firm which made "cigar-store Indians" at the time has no record of filling such an order, and no one has come forward with any information.

The plant has steam pumping engines; the tower is to lift the water to a height that would supply sufficient pressure.

Now, with almost two hundred thousand customers instead of five hundred, the new plant is run by electricity but the old place remains as a stand-by source of power for emergency use and is tested once a year.

Caroline Williams

First Unitarian Church

THE FIRST UNITARIAN CHURCH stands on tree-shaded York Street. The sedate, stone building will soon be one hundred years old, one of the oldest buildings in the neighborhood, predating the Library across the way by almost forty years.

The congregation goes back to 1830 when the First Unitarian Society of Louisville was formed. Their first building was at Fifth and Walnut where the Kentucky Hotel now stands.

In 1871, when the present fine church on York Street was dedicated, the name was changed to the "Church of the Messiah," a title used for over forty years before being changed back to the First Unitarian.

Today the church is one of the many in the neighborhood, their spires rising in classic beauty above the rooftops of the surrounding houses.

The City Hall

THERE WAS very little construction right after the Civil War. Nothing elaborate was undertaken, just simple buildings, necessary for existence. Then, by 1870, the population soared over the hundred thousand mark, and the city began looking forward, started to move again. The famous Galt House had burned to the ground and a new hotel, costing a million dollars, was under construction. The first bridge over the Ohio was completed and Louisville started work on its City Hall.

In 1866 there had been a five hundred dollar prize contest for the best design for the civic building and now the winner, John Andrewartha, started with his project.

Three years were spent on the construction. At the cost of less than half a million the building was finally finished—an elaborate, post-bellum, French Renaissance City Hall—adorned with interesting relief sculpture including pigs, cows and horses over the windows. It is fanciful, delightful and typical of the profuse ornamentation of the times.

The picturesque qualities of the massive building have been more or less overlooked because of the age and beauty of the Courthouse next door but as the years go by it is beginning to receive a little more attention.

The Belle of Louisville

A RIVERTOWN needs a steamboat to symbolize her past and Louisville has the *Belle*. The popular excursion boat, all remodeled and gay, now docks down on the riverfront at a spot once noisy with steam whistles and clanking bells, when as many as eight such craft jammed the wharfs at one time. That was the golden day when a town's prosperity was measured by the traffic of the boats, and newspapers carried columns filled with their scheduled comings and goings. It was the time when the floating palaces were supreme; a day of swaying hoop skirts, gamblers, high silk hats, and calliopes. It was the era that followed in the wake of the first steamboat built—the *Orleans*—that stopped by Louisville for the first time around midnight one autumn night in 1811.

The *Belle of Louisville* recaptures a moment of that period in history for the present generation. She is the last of the authentic stern wheeler excursion boats. With giant paddle wheel and loud calliope and a top speed of ten miles an hour she has won her popularity and become part of the summertime scene on the water.

The boat was built in 1914 and started life under the name of the *Idlewild*, then traveled all over the inland waterways as the *Avalon*, an excursion boat. The city bought her at auction in 1962 when she was old and tired and brought her home to start a new and pampered life.

Main Street

MAIN STREET is a proud old thoroughfare—justly proud. As the name implies, this was the main street of the old town—the first back from the river—the important commercial and business section.

Now, in the name of progress, the buildings are being demolished one by one. It will be a sad day when they all disappear, for there are buildings along here that are beauties, and there is craftsmanship that will never be duplicated again.

The builders took pride in their creations, the owners pride in the façades they presented to the world. Individuality ruled. The space, for the footage was expensive, was sometimes limited but marble, limestone, cast-iron filigree, decorated the exteriors in abundance. Imagination and variegated design was the rule as these representatives of a golden, happy day in Louisville's history were built along old Main Street.

Caroline Williams

The Public Library

From FOURTH STREET, a fountain plays against the side of the great new Public Library which opened in September of 1969. The new building, with its red carpets, airy spaciousness and very modern facilities, stands back to back with the long-familiar quarters on York Street that had served the public since its dedication in 1908.

The very first city library was chartered a hundred years ago when enough money was raised through a series of lotteries to buy the Weisiger Hall, where Kaufman's now stands, and fill the shelves with a collection of fifty thousand books. A few years later the Polytechnic Society took over and directed the operations until, at the turn of the century, the Kentucky Legislature created the Louisville Free Public Library.

Bank of the United States

As in every pioneer community, the earliest citizens of Louisville found that barter and trade served their needs for a while and no uniform money system was needed. Land warrants, signed over to new owners, were as good as gold, furs were accepted for whiskey and food, bits and pieces of eastern money and Spanish coins passed from hand to hand. And, as usual, an entrepreneur or two soon became human clearing houses, giving receipts for furs, whiskey and tobacco that were readily honored by others. It is said that a flatboat on the river front finally emerged as the central exchange post, giving certificates for future payment of goods received that were as good as any paper money could be. Then came small, private banks, in homes or connected with other businesses.

In 1828 the city was incorporated, with a population of ten thousand governed by a mayor and aldermen. Three years later the canal was finished. The city was growing up. In 1832 the Government built the small brick bank, still standing on Main Street, to house the Louisville Branch of the Bank of the United States. It was the first building in the city built solely as a bank and the first Federal Building in town. A few years later it became the Bank of Kentucky. It is now an interesting office building, serving the Life Insurance Company of Kentucky.

United Artists Theatre

THE MOST BIZARRE building on Fourth Street is the United Artists Theatre, whose too-fancy facade stands out among those of the more modest structures like a bit of make-believe.

The overly decorative place is a remnant of the fabulous 1920s, when "moving pictures" were at the height of their days of glory and the palaces in which they were shown matched the unreality, the illusion of splendor, displayed in the films. Built as Loew's Theatre, this movie mecca was designed by John Eberson, considered by many the best architect in the field. He graduated from the nickname "Opera House John," and created about one hundred of the gaudiest, the most fantastic of all the lavish movie houses. This one, both inside and out, is typical of his unrestrained imagination.

The building represents a period in history as remote from present-day taste and style as do the relics of the frontier days. It stands as part of an era of gilt-edge exuberance that may never come again, and deserves a place in the records of the city's growth.

Caroline Williams

The Medical Institute

THIS GRAND OLD BUILDING on Chestnut at Eighth stands neglected, rather forlorn, with windows broken and urban renewal all around, but it holds a place in the history of higher education in Louisville. This is where it began.

In 1837 this block of Chestnut, between Eighth and Ninth, was set aside by the city as the site for a college and designated as College Square by those early city fathers who felt the need for higher education. The best of the architects, Gideon Shryock, designed the building and it opened as home of the Medical Institute. This is the school which combined with Louisville College to form the university—making it the oldest municipally owned university in America.

Central Presbyterian Church

For DIGNITY AND BEAUTY, the Central Presbyterian Church can not be equalled in town. Built some years ago at Fourth and Kentucky, it is one of the churches now trying to keep the inroads of commercial enterprises from changing the residential character of the surrounding neighborhood.

The Presbyterians did not have the first church in Louisville but they did have the most pretentious of the very early buildings. Built in 1816, it had a tower and a bell. Since it was the only bell in town, it was used as the curfew, ringing at ten o'clock at night and again at dawn. It also served as the fire alarm.

That was the First Presbyterian Church which later changed its name to the Central Presbyterian. In 1898 it consolidated with the College Street congregation to form the Fourth Avenue membership.

Caroline Williams

Filson Club

Since 1929 the large, distinguished looking, red brick building on Breckinridge has served as the home of the Filson Club. It was organized in 1884 when ten men gathered together with a common interest in Kentuckiana, and has been collecting items on all aspects of local history every since.

Pioneer relics, mementos, books, pamphlets, clippings and manuscripts are on file in the spacious quarters, making it one of the finest Historical Societies in the country, known as the place to contact for authentic facts concerning the State.

The Club was named for John Filson, Kentucky's first historian. He was also a school teacher and mapmaker, an interesting pioneer who was presumed to have been killed by the Indians when he disappeared into the forests along the Miami River while on a surveying trip in Ohio. He is credited with creating the short-lived name of "Losantiville" for the town, across from the Licking, that later became Cincinnati.

Caroline Williams

Shakertown

THE RESTORATION of Shakertown, a short drive from the city, has given weary city-dwellers an opportunity to step back into a quiet bit of the past. In the small village, known as Pleasant Hill, twenty five of the original buildings still stand, built by that interesting religious group, the Shakers, now extinct, that quietly practiced its beliefs in celibacy, separation from the world and community of goods.

It was a prosperous, thrifty settlement, isolated from the surrounding countryside by its religion, containing some five hundred inhabitants around the middle of the last century. Among their interesting buildings, all simple in design, austere and sturdy is the Center Family Dwelling House with its twin entrances and separate stairways, built of Kentucky River limestone. Nearby is the Farm Deacon's Shop, built in 1809 and the oldest permanent building in Pleasant Hill.

Pleasure Boats

LITTLE HARBORS dot the Ohio on both sides as each summer more and more people take to the water. Pleasure boats of every size and description anchor at the water's edge and weekend commodores bask in the sun and enjoy the river.

Once the River was used just as a means of transportation, the main highway for the pioneers, carrying the keel boats and flatboats downstream. Then came the steamboats, carrying all the cargo, offering the best mode of travel. The going was slow but roads were few and travel over the dusty, rough surfaces even slower.

Now with all the many miles of concrete highways, travel on land is fast—and nerve-shattering. Weekenders and vacationists turn back to the slower pace and the peaceful quiet of the river for relaxation.

Caroline Williams